W9-BLB-816

SAPPHICS AGAINST ANGER
AND OTHER POEMS

Random House
New York

SAPPHICS AGAINST ANGER

and Other Poems

TIMOTHY STEELE

Grateful acknowledgment is made to the following
publications, in which some of these poems (in
certain cases, in slightly different versions) first
appeared: *Canto, Chicago Review, Gramercy Review,
Greensboro Review, Nebo, Occident, Paris Review,
Pushcart Prize, VIII, Sequoia, Southern Review,
Threepenny Review*, and *TriQuarterly*. "Angel,"
"Chanson Philosophique," "The Chorus," and "On
the Eve of a Birthday" were initially published in
Poetry, copyright 1982 and 1983 by the Modern
Poetry Association.

"Waiting for the Storm" was first printed as a
broadside by Victoria Steele at the Horn Press in
the Lawrence Clark Powell Library at UCLA. Other
poems appeared in the following limited editions:
The Prudent Heart (Symposium Press), *Nine
Poems* (R. L. Barth), *On Harmony* (Abattoir
Editions), and *Short Subjects* (R. L. Barth).

The author wishes to thank the Guggenheim
Foundation for a fellowship which enabled him to
complete this collection.

Library of Congress Cataloging-in-Publication Data
Steele, Timothy.
Sapphics Against Anger and Other Poems
I. Title.
PS3569.T33845S2   1986   811'.54   86-462
ISBN 0-394-55803-0
ISBN 0-394-74287-7 (pbk.)

Manufactured in the United States of America
98765432
First Edition

Typography by J. K. Lambert

DEDICATION

for Vikram Seth

We enter life and thus inherit
The kingdom of the human voice.
The Word is Word because we share it.
Wonder encourages our choice
To sort out life's conflicting data,
To come to terms with its traumata,
To shape ourselves to nothing less
Than reasoned self-forgetfulness.
For years we've traded rhyme and measure,
And if our poems are books today,
It is in hopes that others may
Take from them solace, sense, or pleasure,
Though years pass with their wonted speed
And though the times we shared recede.

CONTENTS

SAPPHICS AGAINST ANGER
AND OTHER POEMS

FROM A ROOFTOP

At dawn, down in the streets, from pavement grills,
Steam rises like the spent breath of the night.
At open windows, curtains stir on sills;
There's caging drawn across a market's face;
An empty crane, at its construction site,
Suspends a cable into chasmed space.

The roof shows other rooftops, their plateaus
Marked with antennas from which lines are tied
And strung with water beads or hung with clothes.
And here and there a pigeon comes to peck
At opaque puddles, its stiff walk supplied
By herky-jerky motions of its neck.

Downtown, tall buildings surmount a thinning haze.
The newest, the world center of a bank,
Has sides swept upward from a block-broad base,
Obsidian glass, fifty stories tall;
Against it hangs a window-washer's plank,
An aerie on a frozen waterfall.

Nearer and eastward, past still-sleeping blocks,
Crews on the waterfront are changing shifts.
Trucks load at warehouses at the foot of docks;
A tug out in the bay, gathering speed,
With a short hollow blast of puffed smoke, lifts
Gulls to a cawing and air-borne stampede.

It is as if dawn pliantly compels
The city to relax to sounds and shapes,
To its diagonals and parallels:
Long streets with traffic signals blinking red,
Small squares of parks, alleys with fire escapes,
Rooftops above which cloudless day is spread.

And it's as if the roofs' breeze-freshened shelves,
Their level surfaces of gravelled tar
Where glassy fragments glitter, are themselves
A measure of the intermediate worth
Of all the stories to the morning star
And all the stories to the morning earth.

THE SHEETS

From breezeway or through front porch screen
You'd see the sheets, wide blocks of white
Defined against a backdrop of
A field whose grasses were a green
　　　Intensity of light.

How fresh they looked there on the line,
Their laundered sweetness through the hours
Gathering richly in the air
While cumulus clouds gathered in
　　　Topheavily piled towers.

We children tightroped the low walls
Along the garden; bush and bough
And the washed sheets moved in the wind;
And thinking of this now recalls
　　　Vasari's tale of how

Young Leonardo, charmed of sight,
Would buy in the loud marketplace
Caged birds and set them free—thus yielding
Back to the air which gave him light
    Lost beauty and lost grace.

So with the sheets: for as they drew
Clear warming sunlight from the sky,
They gave to light their rich, clean scent.
And when, the long day nearly through,
    My cousin Anne and I

Would take the sheets down from the line,
We'd fold in baskets their crisp heat,
Absorbing, as they had, the fine
Steady exchange of earth and sky,
    Material and sweet.

SNAPSHOTS FOR POSTERITY

Already the infant
Has turned towards
Those grandly situated
Between memory
And anticipation—
Past and future—upon
The moving edge of time.

O little sausage legs,
Unsteadily
Padding the floor,
You pause,
And your fingers clutch
And release the air
In unblinking wonderment.

May you one day chant,
"Vanity, vanity,"
As a charm against
The chartering of hopes,

The illusory ports
Of wares and commerce.
Then, lucky child,

Even shutting the album
Upon the past will be
An act of devotion,
A paternoster
Accommodating
The fluid present,
Apt in all circumstance.

OLD LETTERS

Old letters are reproaches, mute petitions
      Unlosable in some desk drawer
Or attic box. Bunched in brown folders, or
In packets tied with ribbon, they speak of
         Now-jettisoned ambitions
And insecurities which passed for love,
And document not times when we were stronger,
But rather climates favorable to
Illusions not illusions any longer.

Thus they appear to warn us to adjust
      Our self-important postures; and
One may, of a warm summer evening, stand
Reading them in a room where gold light falls,
        In shafts aswim with dust,
Across a floor to flowery-papered walls;
And as one reads, one may, between the lines,
Construct the features of a former self
Too given to the self and its designs.

Likewise, to return the letters finally
      Back to wherever they belong
Is to admit how much of life's gone wrong
Because of vanity and discontent,
            And is as well to envy
Those who refuse to hunger for event
And who accept the wisely-unbegun,
Just wishing decently to get through life
And trying not to injure anyone.

SMALL LIVES

Having explored the oddly solar weather
Inside a lampshade, the dazed fly will tire,
Drop to the desk, and rub front legs together
As though to warm itself before a fire.

Capsizing with a shovelful of peat,
A pill bug wobbles on its back with fear:
It works its numerous and frantic feet,
Then curls its segments up into a sphere.

The topsoil or the manuscript can wait:
I plant my spade or break off in mid-phrase.
If asked why such small lives so fascinate,
Why I observe them, I can't really tell.
But a responsive impulse moves my gaze,
An impulse I can see in them as well.

MOCKINGBIRD

Erratically, tirelessly, in song,
He does his imitations all day long.
Appropriating every voice he hears,
Astonishingly shifting vocal gears,
He chirrups, trills, and whistles crazily,
Perched at the twiggy apex of his tree.

When argued with by smaller, lesser birds,
He raucously refutes them with their words;
When not receiving notice, as he should,
From earthbound members of the neighborhood,
He drops down onto chimney or garage,
Continuing his hectoring barrage.

One might object to his inflated noise,
The pertinacious manner he employs,
Except the sequences which he invents
Are born of urgent pathos, in this sense:
For all his virtuosity of tone,
The singer has no note which is his own.

JANET

Wading away from shore,
We skirt a cloud of midges.
A small-scale desert floor,
The bottom is a smoothed
Expanse of wavy ridges,
Occasionally cross-grooved

Where a clam's left its path.
We scoop from the calm lake
A brisk adaptive bath,
My legs like milky stalks
In water, and a wake
Spreading where Janet walks.

We're twelve and evening leaves
Me edgy and nonplussed:
Her tight red swimsuit sheathes
Slim hips, small breasts, and serves
To shape a figure just
Developing its curves.

The lake's inched up our suits.
Drawing a breath of air,
She sinks, frog kicks, and shoots
Sleekly across the sand,
Beneath the surface where
Her hair was briefly fanned.

LIFE PORTRAIT

thinking of Dora Spenlow and David Copperfield

Her pensive figure charms, as does the lisp
And coaxing baby talk she sometimes plies.
Yet his devotion wanes. What beckons him?
    The customary will-o'-the-wisp—
A dreamed-up soul mate, beautiful and wise?
No matter: what it comes to, in the end,
Is that when in mock-plaintive moments she
Says, "Don't forget, bad boy, your little friend,"
He fails to catch the import of the plea.

She dies; in time he marries his ideal,
And forges to success. Yet the detail
Of his fulfillment never quite convinces.
    And it's her presence he will feel
Hiking up switchbacks of a mountain trail.
The daffodil, bowed at the canyon's rim,
Will drop a bead of water like a note
From its toy trumpet blossom, his eyes will swim,
And he'll feel a thick hot tightness in his throat.

He's one, now, with the greedy overreachers.
She sat, hands on his shoulder, chin on them,
Then ran a thoughtful finger down his profile,
    As if to remind him of his features.
Height shows the small lake as a sparkling gem,
And shows as threads the streams that spill and bend
And join and part along the valley's floor.
He once forgot, bad boy, his little friend,
Although he won't forget her any more.

SAPPHICS AGAINST ANGER

Angered, may I be near a glass of water;
May my first impulse be to think of Silence,
Its deities (who are they? do, in fact, they
       Exist? etc.).

May I recall what Aristotle says of
The subject: to give vent to rage is not to
Release it but to be increasingly prone
       To its incursions.

May I imagine being in the *Inferno*,
Hearing it asked: "Virgilio mio, who's
That sulking with Achilles there?" and hearing
       Virgil say: "Dante,

That fellow, at the slightest provocation,
Slammed phone receivers down, and waved his arms like
A madman. What Attila did to Europe,
       What Genghis Khan did

To Asia, that poor dope did to his marriage."
May I, that is, put learning to good purpose,
Mindful that melancholy is a sin, though
        Stylish at present.

Better than rage is the post-dinner quiet,
The sink's warm turbulence, the streaming platters,
The suds rehearsing down the drain in spirals
        In the last rinsing.

For what is, after all, the good life save that
Conducted thoughtfully, and what is passion
If not the holiest of powers, sustaining
        Only if mastered.

Forest-swelled winds, all night, surge round
The cabin; hugely, trees go wild
Above deep-troughed, snow-drifted ground.
Inside, in front of the fireplace,
Firelight on his stubbled face
And long-sleeved undershirt, the man
Watches his wife, whose woolen form
Bends to the cradle of a child
Wailing against each blast of storm.

Nor can the child be comforted.
He cannot guess the storm will end
Or that in time he will be led
To the mad variousness of hope.
He cannot know of spring's green slope
Or mountain woods where mild winds carry
Full-leafed and many-voiced directives,
And where his own sons will descend
To fertile, river-led perspectives.

NEAR OLYMPIC

West Los Angeles

The neighborhood, part Japanese and part
Chicano, wears its poverty like art
Exotic in its motley oddities.
Over dirt driveways hang banana trees;
In front of small square stucco houses bloom
Broad jacarandas whose rain-washed perfume
At morning half redeems the rush-hour released
Swelled roaring of the freeway six blocks east.
Along the street sit Fords and Oldsmobiles,
Lowslung and ancient; or—with raised rear wheels
And sides flame-painted—Mustangs and Chevelles.
And in the courtyards of one-time motels
In which the poorer families live, there grow
Sweet corn and yellow squash, and chickens go
Jerkily here and there, loud squawkings borne
Through limp, arched iris leaves and stalks of corn.

This, too, a neighborhood of nurseries
And of good gardeners. Walking by, one sees
Behind a block of chest-high chain link fence,
In plastic round containers, succulents;
In small green boxes, blue forget-me-nots;
Ivies whose tendrils rise, staked, from glazed pots
In a sharp polish of small leafy claws;
Fresh hothouse orchids with their pelican jaws;
In tubs of earth, tangerine trees whose fruit
Hangs orangely pendulous, bright, and minute.
And ranged against the main garage's wall,
On shelves of blond boards and red bricks, are all
The bonsai: a one-foot, gold-wired pine,
Thick as a blacksmith's forearm, with a fine
Spray of huge needles; a squat, mossy oak,
Contorted as if by a thunderstroke;
A bougainvillaea massed with densities
Of pinkish blossoms and smooth, pointed leaves.
And over the front gate, a large sign says,
THE WORLD OF PLANTS—
        SUSHAWA AND MENDEZ,
The latter (a bandana handkerchief
Around his head) forever barking brief
Orders into an outdoor phone, burlesque
And confirmation of the picturesque.

Yet when at five the nursery Edens close,
Even the most naïve would not suppose
This place an Eden. Golden-dusked L.A.—
Bright flow of everywhere—goes its own way,
While here, convening in their curbside league,
Young men drink beer, a day of the fatigue
Of idleness behind them. Acid rock
Blasts from a nearby van, but sound can't shock
Those who've long heard it from their lethargy.
And in a yard with a dead pepper tree,
Some meager birds-of-paradise, and dirt,
A child grips balance at her mother's skirt.
A cat paws a toy soldier that it's found,
Prone at attention, on the width of ground
Running with cracks between the walk and street.
One of the young men rises to his feet,
Ready, and also ready not, to leave,
His Camels folded in his T-shirt's sleeve—
Carlos, chief dude of the rec center, slow
Hands in his pockets, mind on Mexico,
As the rich purple evening sky defines
A crescent moon above the power lines.

This is the hour of casual casualties.
Birds clatter in the stiff fronds of palm trees,
The bustle that the twilight's always fed.
The mother strokes her daughter's jet black head;
The child makes choppy trooper steps toward the walk.
Some older children bike along the block,
A girl there crying, *No one catches me*,
Glancing back quickly, pumping furiously
Off from the others. Bent to handlebars,
Only one boy pursues her. Past parked cars,
It's *No one catches me*, and nearly night.
No eyes are following the girl's delight—
At least not Carlos's or the young mother's.
Nor do their eyes meet, ever, one another's.
It is as if they do not see or hear.
The mother will be nineteen come next year,
And Carlos twenty. What they are survives
The limpid vacancies of air, their lives
Now like some urgent, unobtrusive thing,
Withdrawn and lovely and diminishing.

NATIVE SYMPATHY

Perhaps it's wise to turn and hope to see
A welcoming expression on a face,
Though reason is a rare commodity,
Though courtesy is hardly commonplace.

For, if rebuffed, the senses still will solve
The fuzzy scent and surface of a peach.
Joys will return; a beachball will revolve
Breeze-prompted colors down a slope of beach.

A sober thought will rise, compelling rest,
Perhaps the thought of all those who've finessed
A little life from local circumstance,

Perhaps the memory (it, too, will do)
Of clouds whose whitely heaped extravagance
Held summer in a looming overview.

GOLDEN AGE

Even in fortunate times,
The nectar is spiked with woe.
Gods are incorrigibly
Capricious, and the needy
Beg in Nineveh or sleep
In paper-gusting plazas
Of the New World's shopping malls.

Meantime, the tyrant battens
On conquest, while advisers,
Angling for preferment, seek
Expedient paths. Heartbroken,
The faithful advocate looks
Back on cities of the plain
And trudges into exile.

And if any era thrives,
It's only because, somewhere,
In a plane tree's shade, friends sketch
The dust with theorems and proofs,

Or because, instinctively,
A man puts his arm around
The shoulder of grief and walks
It (for an hour or an age)
Through all its tears and telling.

THE WARTBURG, 1521-22

where Luther hides for ten months
after the Diet of Worms

The garden where he broods is like a riddle.
    The circle of the gravel walk,
The sundial which is stationed in the middle,
    A poppy on its hairy stalk:
These are like clues from which may be inferred
Imperatives of the Almighty's Word.

And nature veils, he thinks, a master plan.
    Where hunters feel the woods grow level,
The hare the two dogs savage is frail Man,
    The two dogs are the Pope and Devil;
And in the wind that courses through the forest,
He hears the pure truth the first angels chorussed.

Odd, how his genius courts expectancy,
    And views life as a text it's read.
Yet others, seeking God in all they see,
    Not finding Him, will claim He's dead,
Or will descry false gods when history slips
Into a fraudulent Apocalypse.

This lies, however, centuries away.
　　The present prospect is of hills,
The garden which he walks in, day by day,
　　Leisure he restlessly fulfills,
While far below the fortress, the cascade
Drifts its cold white breath through the gorge's shade.

If everything's arranged, then even doubt
　　Is simply a predestined mood;
And thus he justifies, as he works out,
　　His theories and his solitude,
Gaining conviction while he frets and grieves
Till, one gray dawn in early March, he leaves.

Even this last scene's ambiguously spliced:
　　The bridge creaks down, he rides across;
His mount's as humble as the mount of Christ;
　　And, see, out there above the Schloss,
A widening band of chimney smoke is curled
Vaguely downwind, toward the modern world.

SHUCKING CORN

He plays the host, concerned with timing.
The guests, though, are the awkward sort:
Moths crashing on the screens and climbing
About in photophilic sport.

He sets the kettle on and tests
A casserole now nearly cooked;
She, on the porch's couch-swing, rests
And sees an ear they overlooked.

And then, the white silk gently torn,
She feeds a paper bag the husk.
He calls her; she holds up the corn,
As if a torch to light the dusk.

ON THE EVE OF A BIRTHDAY

As my Scotch, spared the water, blondly sloshes
About its tumbler, and gay manic flame
Is snapping in the fireplace, I grow youthful:
I realize that calendars aren't truthful
And that for all of my grand unsuccesses
External causes are to blame.

And if at present somewhat destitute,
I plan to alter, prove myself more able,
And suavely stroll into the coming years
As into rooms with thick rugs, chandeliers,
And colorfully pyramided fruit
On linened lengths of table.

At times I fear the future won't reward
My failures with sufficient compensation,
But dump me, aging, in a garret room
Appointed with twilit, slant-ceilinged gloom
And a lone bulb depending from a cord
Suggestive of self-strangulation.

Then, too, I have bad dreams, in one of which
A cowled, scythe-bearing figure beckons me.
Dark plains glow at his back: it seems I've died,
And my soul, weighed and judged, has qualified
For an extended, hyper-sultry hitch
Down in eternity.

Such fears and dreams, however, always pass.
And gazing from my window at the dark,
My drink in hand, I'm jauntily unbowed.
The sky's tiered, windy galleries stream with cloud,
And higher still, the dazed stars thickly mass
In their long Ptolemaic arc.

What constellated powers, unkind or kind,
Sway me, what far preposterous ghosts of air?
Whoever they are, whatever our connection,
I toast them (toasting also my reflection),
Not minding that the words which come to mind
Make the toast less toast than prayer:

Here's to the next year, to the best year yet;
To mixed joys, to my harum-scarum prime;
To auguries reliable and specious;
To times to come, such times being precious,
If only for the reason that they get
Shorter all the time.

NIGHT PIECE

Always the same voice
(And what voice pray tell?)
Sings me from sleep.

And when I tender the insomniac's complaints,
It points out the universe
Isn't sleeping, why should I
Expect more than this obscure interval
In which to read by this tensor light,
Stick-figured, jointed at the waist,
Its luminous, bowed head in an old-fashioned bonnet.

Strengthen the weak, cheer the downhearted,
Remember kindnesses received
Rather than injuries endured
(Always the same voice),
Forget not benefits,
Among which, yea, are numbered even
These terrors of the dark.

How gigantic the dark,
How hopeful the litany.

THE LADY OF BRIGHT COUNSEL

". . . a discussion of Love that I heard from a
Mantinean woman called Diotima, who was wise in
this and many other matters."

PLATO, *Symposium,* 201D

It seems to her strange that the mind should observe
The very processes of which it's part.
And no less does a second thought unnerve:
Just when we get our bearings, we must start
To leave the much-in-little that enchants—
The two-way traffic of a file of ants,
The field of birds who chase, dive, or retire
To linear order on a span of wire.

Though doubtful, touching a responsive chord,
She sees beyond confusion after all.
By understating it, she's underscored
Her lesson: when the love we have will fall
To other women and to other men,
It will inspire us to life again.

SHORT SUBJECTS

for my sister Martha, who likes epigrams

1. Skull at the Crossroads

Disparage, if you will, the life you live:
It's preferable to the alternative.

2. Votaries of Cupid

Together five minutes—and we're ashen
With wrath and mutual disgust.
Lovers should glow, love, with their passion,
Not spontaneously combust.

3. Apology

You ask if you may see a sample
Of what I'm working on—but, Ample,
If I comply, then you feel free
To shower your latest work on me,
Petitioning evaluation.
Though not of cynical persuasion,
I feel your interest in my art
Is that I'll take up, for my part,

An interest in your own. To share
One's labor is, I'm well aware,
An act to which even gods descend.
It is an act which I commend;
It is an act which I can savor—
But not when you return the favor.

4. Young American Poets Handicap

All have his praise at the beginning.
He watches us pound round the course,
Happily assured of winning
Because he's bet on every horse.

5. Matthew 5:15

Self-deprecating, you defer
In ways we're called on to admire:
Your lamp beneath a bushel, Sir,
Your object is to cause a fire.

6. Social Reform

A prince of rational behavior,
Satan informs us that our Savior
Remarks we'll always have the poor,
Which moral saves expenditure.
We'll always have the poor? Okay.
Yet, looked at whole, the text will say
Something more lenitive, and truer.
We'll have the poor: let's make them fewer.

7. An L.A. Impromptu

Now this beau draws you, and that one estranges.
You're on and off romantic interchanges
With such gear-grinding, reflex-wrought decision
That it's a miracle there's no collision
Among the men who, over you and under,
Pursue you in a kind of heated wonder
Until you've stickshifted off and dismissed them.
You haven't a lovelife, you've a freeway system.

8. Natural History

He pours forth his fierce, quarrelsome twaddle;
If others speak, he's loath to hear.
Had men evolved along his model,
They'd have two mouths and but one ear.

9. At the Corner of the Counter of the Diner

Its size one trillionth of a proton,
This universe which theorists dote on
Burst out, it seems, in THE BIG BANG.
As if a sort of boomerang,
The whole affair—its stars and spaces,
Its quasars, quarks, and eating places—
May one day seek to reassume
The compact quarters of its womb
And may by violent recensions
Collapse back to its first dimensions.
This would, it seems, be THE BIG CRUNCH,
The merest thought of which spoils lunch.

10. Mirror for Morning

My razor's harvested its foam.
One hand, like upward calipers,
Measures my chin, and, like a comb,
The other rumplingly confers
Some order on my rebel locks.
A face a mother could resist?
Yes, and a source of paradox,
Fertile (down to his very socks)
Material for the satirist.

11. Family Album

I turn a page. At once, breathtakingly,
You hold me sadly, steadily, in view.
Is it because you can't return to me,
Or is it that I'm journeying to you?

LAST TANGO

It is disquieting, that film
In which the plagued protagonist
Won't tell his lover who he is.
It's not just that she turns on him
Or that his youth and age consist
Primarily of chances missed:
The most disturbing thing's that he,
Who loses all else, cannot lose
His own identity.

All life conspires to define us,
Weighing us down with who we are,
Too much drab pain. It is enough
To make one take sides with Plotinus:
Sweet Universal Avatar,
Make me pure spirit, an ensouled star—
Or something slightly less divine:
Rain on an awning, or wind rough
Among clothes on a line.

Of course, it wouldn't do to flee
All longings, griefs, despairs, and such.
Blisses anonymously pursued
Destroy us or, evasively,
Both yield to and resist our touch.
The Brando figure learns as much:
A wholly personal collapse
Succeeds his nameless interlude.
One thinks, though, that perhaps

In some less fallen world, an ease
Might grace our necessary fictions.
There, our identities would be
Like—what?—like Haydn's symphonies,
Structures of balanced contradictions,
For all their evident restrictions,
Crazy with lightness and desire:
La Passione, Mercury,
Tempesta, Mourning, Fire.

IN THE KING'S ROOMS

David, at Mahanaim during the Rebellion

This evening I pace chambers where I sought
To charm an old king with a shepherd's song.
Now I am king, and aging. I once thought
I could forever dwell in quiet caught
From melodies I crafted. I was wrong.

Young, loved by all, I lived beyond all doubt.
I calmed the trembling flank and frightened eye
Of the young doe—and later, led the rout
Of the invaders, lifting with a shout
The giant's head up to an answering sky.

Despised now even by my son, I raise
No shout to heaven. An uncertain friend,
A faithless leader, I can only gaze
Across a land which lent me, once, its praise
And which tonight I grudgingly defend.

Let my smooth, artful counselors secure
Victories in the name of faith and truth.
I can no longer care. Nor am I sure
Whom I should pray forgiveness for—
The old man misled or the too-favored youth.

TIMOTHY

Although the field lay cut in swaths,
Grass at the edge survived the crop:
Stiff stems, with lateral blades of leaf,
Dense cattail flower-spikes at the top.

If there was breeze and open sky,
We raked each swath into a row;
If not, we took the hay to dry
To the barn's golden-showering mow.

The hay we forked there from the truck
Was thatched resilience where it fell,
And I took pleasure in the thought
The fresh hay's name was mine as well.

Work was a soothing, rhythmic ache;
Hay stuck where skin or clothes were damp.
At length, the pick-up truck would shake
Its last stack up the barn's wood ramp.

Pumping a handpump's iron arm,
I washed myself as best I could,
Then watched the acres of the farm
Draw lengthening shadows from the wood

Across the grass, which seemed a thing
In which the lonely and concealed
Had risen from its sorrowing
And flourished in the open field.

CHANSON PHILOSOPHIQUE

The nominalist in me invents
A life devoid of precedents.
The realist takes a different view:
He claims that all I feel and do
Billions of others felt and did
In history's Pre-me period.

Arguing thus, both voices speak
A partial truth. I am unique,
Yet the unceasing self-distress
Of desire buffets me no less
Than it has other sons of man
Who've come and gone since time began.

The meaning, then, of this dispute?
My life's a nominal/real pursuit,
Which leaves identity clear and blurred,
In which what happens has occurred
Often and never—which is to say,
Never to me, or quite this way.

THE TREATISE ON HARMONY

School out, children come through the gate,
Behind them the playground's pavement
With its painted circles and squares,
Its intersections of pastimes.
Boys whistle and call, two duelling
With imaginary swords, thrust
And parry, one advancing, one
Backing, while a girl at the curb

Cranes to see Is the bus coming,
And another, serious in
Blue-bowed pigtails and sailor's blouse,
Leads a younger friend by the hand.
At the children's approach, sparrows
Foraging the walk spurt up to
And through the lozenges of space
Formed by links of the playground fence,

And trees crisply shake themselves, leaves
And the voices beneath them like,
Almost, an orchestra tuning,
Woodwinds, violins, the courtly
Emphasis of a kettledrum,
Confused sound promising music
Expressive of youth, contentious
Or firmly ordered, glad and grave.

JACARANDA

for Sumiye and Dick Kobashigawa

Higher than the camellia trees,
Among whose leaves pine needles land,
The jacaranda's ferns are fanned
In the yard's docile resident breeze.

I read and watch in shifting light.
A small bug, purposeful, unwary,
Explores a page's printed prairie,
And as I turn it, takes to flight.

Impatiens, modestly profuse,
Bloom by a fence, along whose boards,
Wedge-pointed, a squirrel deftly fords
A child's slant M's and W's.

And at a lattice of bamboo,
With trailing strings of bleeding hearts,
A hummingbird appears, hangs, darts,
Sinks, and then vanishes from view.

I see, too, on a phone line, rock
Some doves whose converse is so sweet,
You'd think harsh words passed through their feet
Might be transformed to gentler talk.

And its trunk buttressed by a pole,
The pepper tree stirs its willowy boughs,
Among which hangs a little house,
Its door a peg and a round hole.

Here a plump short-billed finch returns.
He perches to survey the yard
With his quick eye, and to regard,
It seems, the jacaranda's ferns,

Which can't be otherwise construed
Than lowly beauty raised aloft,
Limberly bowed about and soft,
To a befitting altitude.

AN AUBADE

As she is showering, I wake to see
A shine of earrings on the bedside stand,
A single yellow sheet which, over me,
Has folds as intricate as drapery
In paintings from some fine old master's hand.

The pillow which, in dozing, I embraced
Retains the salty sweetness of her skin;
I sense her smooth back, buttocks, belly, waist,
The leggy warmth which spread and gently laced
Around my legs and loins, and drew me in.

I stretch and curl about a bit and hear her
Singing among the water's hiss and race.
Gradually the early light makes clearer
The perfume bottles by the dresser's mirror,
The silver flashlight, standing on its face,

Which shares the corner of the dresser with
An ivy spilling tendrils from a cup.
And so content am I, I can forgive
Pleasure for being brief and fugitive.
I'll stretch some more, but postpone getting up

Until she finishes her shower and dries
(Now this and now that foot placed on a chair)
Her fineboned ankles, and her calves and thighs,
The pink full nipples of her breasts, and ties
Her towel up, turban-style, about her hair.

SUMMER

Voluptuous in plenty, summer is
Neglectful of the earnest ones who've sought her.
She best resides with what she images:
Lakes windless with profound sun-shafted water;
Dense orchards in which high-grassed heat grows thick;
The one-lane country road where, on his knees,
A boy initials soft tar with a stick;
Slow creeks which bear flecked light through depths of trees.

And he alone is summer's who relents
In his poor enterprisings; who can sense,
In alleys petal-blown, the wealth of chance;
Or can, supine in a deep meadow, pass
Warm hours beneath a moving sky's expanse,
Chewing the sweetness from long stalks of grass.

WAITING FOR THE STORM

Breeze sent a wrinkling darkness
Across the bay. I knelt
Beneath an upturned boat,
And, moment by moment, felt

The sand at my feet grow colder,
The damp air chill and spread.
Then the first raindrops sounded
On the hull above my head.

AT WILL ROGERS BEACH

1

Among the swells, the storm past, surfers sit,
    Lifting and sinking in and out of view.
On the horizon, ranged clouds counterfeit
    An Orient Alps; sunlight plunges through
Loose standing billows, and the waves' swift wash
Shoots in with bubblingly confused panache,
      Encircling, as it seethes, a melting fort
        Topped with cup-molded turrets of dark sand,
      While small sandpipers zigzag in a sort
        Of shoulder-hunched brigade along the strand.

2

The aisle of autumn sunlight settling on
    The mobile corrugations of the sea
Fragments and forms at once, is here and gone,
    A durable, elusive energy:
Pure presence and repose—mere lovely being,
To feel which is as natural as seeing
    The dog that dashes up the beach and back

Or, to a pair of onlookers' applause,
Goes skidding to a posture of attack
    And leaps to snatch a Frisbee in his jaws.

3

A man wades with a fishing rod and pail
    Across the soft sand, over which a kite
Makes snapping loops as it pursues its tail.
    One notes gulls weaving at a breezy height
And the lithe power of the tide's advance,
But notes as well the berm's small jousting lance
        (A plastic drink top run through with a straw),
            The fissure where the berm's sand crust has cracked,
        And shingle pebbles which, when waves withdraw,
            Perform their clattering, scraping tumbling act.

4

The wind dies, and the cloud Alps disappear,
    And where the sun now sets, the sky's so swirled
With smoky colors that the atmosphere
    Seems like the abstract beauty of the world.
The swells more regular, there floats at rest
A pelican, long beak tucked to its chest.
        Holding torpedo-shaped red rescue buoys,
            Two lifeguards chat, as surfers, one by one,
        Stagger in through the shallows' mist and noise
            Or paddle back out for a final run.

5

What this abundance means, one cannot say.
    One merely wants to shelter it from harm;
One merely sees the waves burst into spray
    Out where the jetty casts its bouldered arm;
One merely feels the heart contract that this
Should all be utterly precarious.
      It's nearly dark, but there's still light enough
        For those—the surfers' landward counterparts—
      Who roller-skate the walk below the bluff,
        Rehearsing their adroit, spontaneous arts.

6

One of them coasts upright, visoring a hand
    To the sun's afterglow, while, smooth performers,
Two others click past a closed hot-dog stand,
    She in a T-shirt, shorts, tights, and leg-warmers,
He in light gym trunks and a netted top;
And where the long wide pavement curves, they drop
    Into a slight crouch and accelerate,
      Cross-stepping, their arms swinging left and right,
      Translating into speed their form and weight
        And dwindling, as they sweep off, into night.

THE CHORUS

Because fate thought us minor, we stood back
While others took their cues on center stage.
We saw them, trembling, spring to an attack
We knew would fail. Then, desperate to assuage
Their horrors when despair supplanted rage,
    We somehow steadied them in the belief
    There was a higher purpose in their grief.

We saw and felt their passions. We can tell
Of Philoctetes' suppurating wound;
How brave, horse-taming Hector stood and fell,
As on the wall old Priam howled and swooned;
Of Palamedes, beaten to the ground
    And stoned with those same tablets, smooth and white,
    With which he had taught men to count and write.

We couldn't save them, and if we wore masks,
It was to hide the bitterest of tears.
To the sensation-seeking voice which asks
For tales of tumult, flashing shields and spears,

We have no answer, standing in arrears
  To those who could not take the paths we urged,
  But met their terrors head on, and were purged.

This friend, that lover, dear comrades-in-arms:
They hold all meaning we were meant to know.
We've closed their eyes the last time. Safe from harms,
They follow courses where the planets go,
And we who live are solaced, for although
  The years have plundered us of strength and youth,
  We served the gods' commands. We spoke the truth.

BUT HOME IS HERE

April has returned
Box scores to the papers,
Scrub jays to the lawn

(How they bounce!—feet forward
Like long-jumpers landing),
And I fix dinner for one.

My arm raised, the egg cracked,
The quick rope of the white
Lowers yoke to mixing bowl,

A seeded hemisphere
Of sliced tomato
Rocking on the cutting board.

The days growing longer,
I sing to the trees,
The flowering pear and persimmon,

To the morning-glories
Which insinuate vines
Through knotholes in the fence:

Life, life, how sad, how rushed
You are, how self-divided,
Cells doubling and parting

Into patterns and flows,
To complication,
To oblivion.

When the cat arches
On my leg, I sweep her up
And hold her above me, pleading,

*Calypso, make me not
Immortal but happy
On earth: send me home.*

Ah, but home is here,
With a salad and omelette,
And the darkness coming

Like a friend, like the hope
Of wisdom arriving,
However late.

ANGEL

At Christmas season, when the tree was trimmed,
I'd lie beneath a ceiling veined and limbed
And splashed with color from the blinking lights.
Not far below the treetop's five-bulb star,
An angel cruised the decorated heights,
Playing a papier-mâché guitar.

I'd hear my brother's crackling radio
And sense the privacy of night and snow.
The living room itself was rearranged
To make way for the tree, sofas and chairs
Moved back against the wall, their aspect changed
By occupying space not usually theirs.

All through that altered Advent atmosphere,
The angel played a strain I couldn't hear,
Perhaps no less melodious for the fact.
The colors soothed, the darkened room was warm;
The angel, if inscrutably abstract,
Appeared designed to hearten and inform.

Sometimes I'd climb a chair and take it down.
It had a flowing, multi-folded gown,
A wave of hair arrested by a wing,
But though its smile comprised a pursed mild line,
Whichever way I turned it on its string,
Its eyes looked elsewhere, never meeting mine.

LOVE POEM

for Victoria

The story's told of speechless Pierrot's
    Defense of his secluded tower.
Beleagured by imaginary foes,
Relying simply on his anxious power,
He would toil up the stairway every night,
Then rush round madly when the moon arose
To drive away the moon's invasive light.

The clutched-at beams always escaped his grasp
    Effortlessly. Distracted wraith!
His hands had nothing but themselves to clasp;
Mute self-absorption was his only faith.
Brave as he was, frustration made him weep,
And balked by force elusive as his breath,
He sank at last into exhausted sleep.

If, like poor Pierrot, I've anxiously
  Dwelt in my life, the spell is broken.
Awakened to your touch and voice, I see
That evil is the formless and unspoken,
And that peace rests in form and nomenclature,
Which render our two natures—formerly
Discomfited, self-conscious—second nature.

THE SKIMMING STONE

in memory of Billy Knight,
who died of a heart attack, age 38

The factory on the river, during lunch
We'd skim stones to a current brown and slow.
The shore was pebbles that our boots would scrunch
As we searched back and forth for stones to throw.
Most of the stones were poor New England slate;
A few had—smooth and round—the proper weight,
And we'd spin off long runs and argue whether
To count concluding skips that merged together.

Once when the whistle called us from the shore,
You pocketed a stone. Was it for luck?
Or did you feel a specially close rapport
That day with life, with youth? Or were you struck
Merely that the stone's smooth warmth implied
A longer rather than a shorter ride?

TOWARD CALGARY

Out over these parched, gusty plains,
Loose dirt is lifted to a sail;
Beyond wide distances, a train's
Smoke draws a horizontal trail.

Posts bear a wire, mile after mile,
Across deep views toward which winds roll,
That wire the only obstacle
Between the winds and the North Pole.

Here one could drive what seems an age,
Seeing no more than levelled land
And, on the road, slow-skidding sage
And skating shapes of wind-blown sand.

Here one could try the radio's dial
And, as the inching needle slips
Through far, infrequent static, feel
A stilled world at the fingertips.

And one might sense nothing but thirst
Or soundless hours in this place
Where all horizons are dispersed
Continuously into space.

Yet from caked, crumbly ground and rocks
The spiky purple lupines grow
And cacti shaped like tuning forks.
And some who've crossed such precincts know

The prudent heart is like these plains,
Where quietness has grown immense,
No landmarks rendering its terrains
Measurable to human sense,

And where, remote of any tree,
The sky is an inclusive drift
Of radiance chastening, endlessly,
Needless invention, needless thrift.